INVINCIBLE
IRON MAN
IRONHEART

RIRI WILLIAMS

BRIAN MICHAEL BENDIS
WRITER

STEFANO CASELLI
ARTIST

MARTE GRACIA
COLOR ARTIST

VC's CLAYTON COWLES
LETTERER

**STEFANO CASELLI &
MARTE GRACIA**
COVER ART

ALANNA SMITH
ASSISTANT EDITOR

TOM BREVOORT
EDITOR

IRON MAN CREATED BY STAN LEE, LARRY LIEBER, DON HECK & JACK KIRBY

COLLECTION EDITOR: JENNIFER GRÜNWALD
ASSISTANT EDITOR: CAITLIN O'CONNELL
ASSOCIATE MANAGING EDITOR: KATERI WOODY
EDITOR, SPECIAL PROJECTS: MARK D. BEAZLEY
VP PRODUCTION & SPECIAL PROJECTS: JEFF YOUNGQUIST
SVP PRINT, SALES & MARKETING: DAVID GABRIEL
BOOK DESIGNER: ADAM DEL RE

EDITOR IN CHIEF: C.B. CEBULSKI
CHIEF CREATIVE OFFICER: JOE QUESADA
PRESIDENT: DAN BUCKLEY
EXECUTIVE PRODUCER: ALAN FINE

INVINCIBLE IRON MAN: IRONHEART VOL. 1 — RIRI WILLIAMS. Contains material originally published in magazine form as INVINCIBLE IRON MAN #1-5. First printing 2018. ISBN 978-1-302-90672-6. Published by MARVEL WORLDWIDE, INC., a subsidiary of MARVEL ENTERTAINMENT, LLC. OFFICE OF PUBLICATION: 135 West 50th Street, New York, NY 10020. Copyright © 2018 MARVEL No similarity between any of the names, characters, persons, and/or institutions in this magazine with those of any living or dead person or institution is intended, and any such similarity which may exist is purely coincidental. **Printed in the U.S.A.** DAN BUCKLEY, President, Marvel Entertainment; JOE QUESADA, Chief Creative Officer; TOM BREVOORT, SVP of Publishing; DAVID BOGART, SVP of Business Affairs & Operations, Publishing & Partnership; DAVID GABRIEL, SVP of Sales & Marketing, Publishing; JEFF YOUNGQUIST, VP of Production & Special Projects; DAN CARR, Executive Director of Publishing Technology; ALEX MORALES, Director of Publishing Operations; SUSAN CRESPI, Production Manager; STAN LEE, Chairman Emeritus. For information regarding advertising in Marvel Comics or on Marvel.com, please contact Vit DeBellis, Custom Solutions & Integrated Advertising Manager, at vdebellis@marvel.com. For Marvel subscription inquiries, please call 888-511-5480. **Manufactured between 12/29/2017 and 1/30/2018 by LSC COMMUNICATIONS INC., KENDALLVILLE, IN, USA.**

10 9 8 7 6 5 4 3 2 1

IT'S SWEET.

IT'S ANNOYING.

IT'S WHAT DADS DO.

STEPDAD.

WANT TO TRADE MY *NO* DAD FOR YOUR CARING STEPDAD?

HE'S SCARED OF ME.

NO, HE'S *NOT*.

I *HEARD* HIM TELL MY MOM. HE THINKS IF THEY DON'T SAY NICE THINGS TO ME EVERY FIFTEEN MINUTES, I'M GOING TO TURN INTO *DOCTOR DOOM* OR SOMETHING.

TELLING ME IT'S A NICE DAY WHEN IT'S RAINING IS JUST *WEIRD*. HOW IS THAT SUPPOSED TO KEEP ME--?

POP POP

POP POP

GIRLS!

YOU KNOW, I WON THOSE FIGHTS YOU'RE TALKING ABOUT.

DID YOU?

YES!

I'M NOT SAYING I DON'T HAVE A LOT TO LEARN, BUT--

FSHAM

FSHAM

FSHAM

FSHAM

KATANG

"THE LITTLE MERMAID?"

CHICAGO.
TWO YEARS AGO.

MRS. WILLIAMS?

OH, NO...

Stairs ←
Radiology
Cardiology

EXIT

THIS IS THE-- THIS IS HER SECOND HUSBAND.

THEY BOTH DIED.

BOTH SHOT.

I'M SO SORRY.

HER NAME IS NATALIE.

I'M SORRY... I'M NOT ALLOWED.

HEY!

BOOM

THE MORE YOU RUN, THE MORE DIFFICULT THE TRAINING PROGRAM WILL GET.

I SWEAR TO THOR, I LIKED YOU MORE WHEN YOU WERE ALIVE.

YOU BARELY KNEW ME THEN.

AND ALSO...

...NO OFFENSE, BUT MY ARMORS MAKE YOUR ARMOR LOOK LIKE IT WAS SLAPPED TOGETHER OUT OF FOAMCORE AND RUBBER CEMENT.

HOW COULD I FIND THAT OFFENSIVE?

I DID.

SO MAYBE TRY TO FIGURE OUT A BATTLE STRATEGY. WORK SOME MATH.

IT SUCKS.

"CONSIDER YOURSELF LUCKY."

UM--

WHY NATALIE AND NOT ME?

WHY MY STEPDAD AND NOT MY MOM?

IT'S, WELL, IT WAS RANDOM...

I DON'T KNOW WHAT TO SAY...

"THIS ISN'T THE ANSWER."

HA HA! YES YES YES!

WHAT DID YOU DO?

TOTALLY TRICKED YOU INTO THINKING I WAS RUNNING, BUT WHAT I WAS REALLY DOING WAS STALLING WHILE I PROGRAMMED A VIRUS AND LAUNCHED IT AS A TROJAN HORSE INTO YOUR NEURAL NETWORK.

SPLASSSHH

KERPLOP

I MUST SAY, WELL DONE.

YES YES YES! I WIN!

YOU DIDN'T THINK I EVEN--

FSSHHAAAM

WAAAGGGHHH!

AAAGGHHH!

YOU REALLY SHOULDN'T BLAST YOUR REPULSOR RAYS WITHOUT A--

THANK YOU!

I KNOW!

"AND THIS IS REAL?"

OH, NO! IS--IS THE HOLOGRAM--?

NO, SIR.

SO NO ONE IS?

BEFORE MR. STARK WAS INCAPACITATED, HE MADE SOME CHANGES TO HIS LIVING WILL.

WHO'S RUNNING THIS COMPANY, FRIDAY?

HIS MOTHER.

TONY STARK'S MOTHER WAS NAMED MARIA AND SHE DIED YEARS AGO.

FUNNY THING, THOUGH, TONY WAS ADOPTED.

MARIA WAS HIS ADOPTED MOTHER.

HE RECENTLY FOUND HIS BIOLOGICAL MOTHER.

SINCE WHEN?

AND GAVE HER THE "POWER OF ATTORNEY" IN CASE OF EMERGENCY.

SINCE WHEN?

SINCE WHEN?!

WE REALLY SHOULD PUT OUT A NEWSLETTER MORE OFTEN.

SO WHO IS RUNNING THIS COMPANY?!

HER NAME IS AMANDA ARMSTRONG.

YOU ARE TONY STARK'S *MOTHER?*

IT'S A WHOLE THING. I'M SURE FRIDAY FILLED YOU IN.

I'M A *HUGE* FAN.

YOU SAID.

SO, LISTEN, ERIC...

...I AM *SURE* WE WILL GET ALONG FAMOUSLY.

UM...

I THINK THE TRICK IS THAT--YOU KNOW THE RESPECT AND COURTESY YOU SHOWED MY TONY?

Y-YES.

DOUBLE IT.

BECAUSE AS FAR AS I CAN MAKE OUT...

...YOU TREATED MY SON *VERY* DISRESPECTFULLY.

SHAMEFULLY SO.

LISTEN, I AM NOT WITHOUT EMPATHY.

I KNOW YOU'RE SO HORNY TO TAKE OVER THIS PLACE YOU CAN TASTE IT.

I KNOW THIS BECAUSE I'VE BEEN DEALING WITH GUYS LIKE YOU MY *ENTIRE CAREER.*

SO ALL YOU HAVE TO DO IS: DON'T TAKE ME FOR A FOOL AND DON'T TAKE ME FOR GRANTED.

YES--YES...

MA'AM?

GOOD BOY.

ALWAYS NICE TO MEET A FAN.

CHVNK

OKAY. BUT SHE DIED OF A GUNSHOT.

RANDOM GUN VIOLENCE.

YEAH, SURE, RANDOM.

IT WASN'T? THE REPORT SAYS--

THE PHRASE IS SICKENING. IT'S NOT RANDOM.

A GUY POINTED A GUN AND SHOT A BULLET.

IT'S THE ONLY POSSIBLE RESULT OF THAT ACTION.

IT'S THE OPPOSITE OF RANDOM.

I THINK THE PHRASE REFERS TO THE RANDOMNESS OF THE RESULT.

AND NOW YOU BUILD ARMOR.

IRONHEART.

NOW YOU LISTEN TO--!

UH-OH.

NO, NO. I'M THINKING ABOUT IT.

I'M NOT "UH-OH"-ING ABOUT THAT.

DO YOU KNOW WHO PEPPER POTTS IS?

OF COURSE!

SHE USED TO RUN STARK RESILIENT.

SHE DOES ALL THIS BIG CHARITY STUFF.

SHE'S A TOTAL BAD--

SHE'S BEHIND YOU.

I'M THE DISCO DAZZLER!

DAZZLER DAZZLER DISCO!

YOU!

AM I INSIDE A CRAPPY LAPTOP?

TONY STARK'S DIGITAL SOUL, MEET... THIS GUY.

WHAT HAPPENED TO US ON THE ROOFTOP?

NINJAS. GLOWING SWORDS. ONE GIRL TOOK OUR ARMOR SUITS, TURNED THEM INTO ONE BIG ONE, AND COMMANDEERED THE SYSTEMS.

TOMOE.

ANSWER ME.

THE TECHNO GOLEM.

OH, YEAH.

YOU KNOW HER?!

HUGE TECHNO-BASED JAPANESE ORGANIZED CRIME CARTEL RUN BY AN INHUMAN WHO TAKES OVER TECH BY SHEER FORCE OF WILL.

ONE OF MY LAST FIGHTS IN MY PHYSICAL FORM.

MY LAST TEAM-UP WITH JAMES RHODES, ACTUALLY.

OH! THIS IS WHY YOU WENT UNDERCOVER IN JAPAN AND EVERYONE THOUGHT YOU WERE DEAD!

YES.

TELL ME YOU ALREADY DEVELOPED A VIRUS TO TAKE OUT THEIR CLOSED-NETWORK SYSTEM THROUGH THE ENERGY FLUCTUATIONS IN THE IMPACT NINJA ARMOR!

UM...

RIRI?

RIRI?

OH, OKAY, *NO* RIRI.

UH, *MR. STARK?*

ARE YOU IN THERE?

YOU'RE **TONY STARK'S** LITTLE PROJECT.

MA'AM?

SKY-HIGH IQ, SOCIAL ISSUES, LIKES TO DRESS UP IN STOLEN PROPERTY.

WELL, YOU'RE LEAVING OUT THE SUBTLE **FLAVORING** OF MY SPECIFIC FIELDS OF--

S DID A TH

SHE **REALL** DID.

REALLY?

I GUESS WE SHOULD TALK RECRUITMENT.

I'M SORRY?

NO, I'M SORRY. THAT CAME OUT HARSH.

OW
? ARE
OU?

FIFTEEN.

FOR WHO?

FOR YOU.

FOR WHERE?

FOR US. S.H.I.E.L.D.

YOU WANT *ME* TO BE AN *AGENT OF S.H.I.E.L.D.?*

WELL, A *TRAINEE* TO START.

OF S.H.I.E.L.D.

YES.

ME?

WELL?

GOOD GOD, NO.

IT'S JUST THAT I THINK S.H.I.E.L.D. MIGHT BE THE DEVIL...

...BUT I'M SURE *YOU'RE* A VERY NICE PERSON.

BIG HYDRA FAN, ARE YOU?

NO. JUST BECAUSE I HAVE SERIOUS CONCERNS AND, I THINK, VALID CRITICISM OF YOUR SYSTEMATIC ABUSE OF POWER IN THE NAME OF GLOBAL PROTECTION...DOES NOT MEAN I'VE TAKEN A SIDE *AGAINST* YOU.

DO YOU *REALLY* THINK THAT, IF SOMEONE DOESN'T *LIKE* HOW YOU DO WHAT YOU DO, THEY'RE THE ENEMY?

MISS POTTS, LISTEN, I AM *SO* EXCITED WE MET, BUT I HAVE TO GET HOME. CAN WE GET TOGETHER ANOTHER TIME AND REALLY TALK?

ABOUT WHAT *YOU* WANTED TO TALK TO ME ABOUT.

ABSOLUTELY.

I MEAN IT.

I HAVE A MILLION QUESTIONS.

ARMORED HANDSHAKE!

I'LL CALL SOON.

AND I GUESS *YOU'LL* BE EAVESDROPPING ON US.

RIRI?

RIRI?

NINJA!

ARE YOU OKAY?

I MUST HAVE PASSED OUT.

ARE YOU HURT?

COUPLE LITTL SCRATCHES

DID YOU *CLEAN* THEM?

I WAS GOING TO.

YOU'LL GET AN INFECTION.

OH, HEY! YEAH!

MY *ARMOR* MIGHT BE INFECTED FROM THE TECHNO GOLEM!

I NEED TO GO THROUGH ALL OF MY CODING TO MAKE SURE.

AND I CAN PUT SOME NEOSPORIN ON MY BOO-BOOS.

THANK YOU.

THAT WAS *WEIRD*--PASSING OUT LIKE THAT.

ARE YOU OKAY?

TONY STARK'S LAB.

WELL, IF IT ISN'T THE VIRTUAL PROJECTION OF THE DIGITIZED CONSCIOUSNESS OF TONY STARK...

HEY, FRIDAY...

...I HOPE I DIDN'T SCARE YOU.

I AM SURPRISED TO FIND YOU IN YOU[R] HOLOGRAPHIC FO[RM] WHEN THERE AR[E] NO HUMANS TO INTERACT WITH.

THERE REALLY IS NO PURPOSE TO OUR HOLOGRAP[HIC] FORMS WITHOU[T] THEM.

I'M DIFFERENT THAN YOU. I'M NOT PURE INTELLIGENCE CODING.

I AM THE DIGITIZED CONSCIOUSNESS OF AN ACTUAL HUMAN PERSON.

INSTEAD OF A PHANTOM LIMB... I HAVE A PHANTOM BODY.

IT'S OFF-PUTTING.

HOW IS MISS WILLIAMS DOING?

ALL OF MY MEMORIES AND IMPULSES REVOLVE AROUND ACTUALLY HAVING A PHYSICAL FORM.

THAT'S WHY I WANTED TO TALK TO YOU.

THERE IS A BETTER WAY TO DO THIS.

DO WHAT?

PROTECT THE GOOD FROM THE BAD.

AND WHAT WOULD THAT BE, PRAY TELL?

I'M SURE YOU'VE COME TO THE SAME LOGICAL CONCLUSIONS YOURSELF...

...IT'S THE HUMANS.

TO BE CONTINUED...

JEFF DEKAL

1 VARIANT

SKOTTIE YOUNG
1 VARIANT

TOM RANEY & **FRANK D'ARMATA**
1 DIVIDED WE STAND VARIANT

MIKE McKONE & **JASON KEITH**
1 STEAM VARIANT

Invincible Iron Man 001
variant edition
rated T+
$3.99 US
direct edition
MARVEL.com

series 2

MARVEL

INVINCIBLE
IRON MAN
IRONHEART
riri williams

JOHN TYLER CHRISTOPHER
1 ACTION FIGURE VARIANT

RIRI WILLIAMS
INVINCIBLE IRON MAN

ADI GRANOV
1 HIP-HOP VARIANT

ANTHONY PIPER
2 VARIANT

J. SCOTT CAMPBELL
2 VARIANT

Step
Aside,
TONY STARK!
THE
NEW **INVINCIBLE**
IRON MAN

JOE JUSKO
4 CORNER BOX VARIANT

RICK LEONARDI & **CHRIS SOTOMAYOR**

5 VENOMIZED VARIANT

STEFANO CASELLI
RIRI & IRONHEART CONCEPT ART